And That's Why She's My Mama

(Positive Affirmations Edition)

This book belongs to

_____

by Tiarra Nazario
illustrated by Gabby Correia

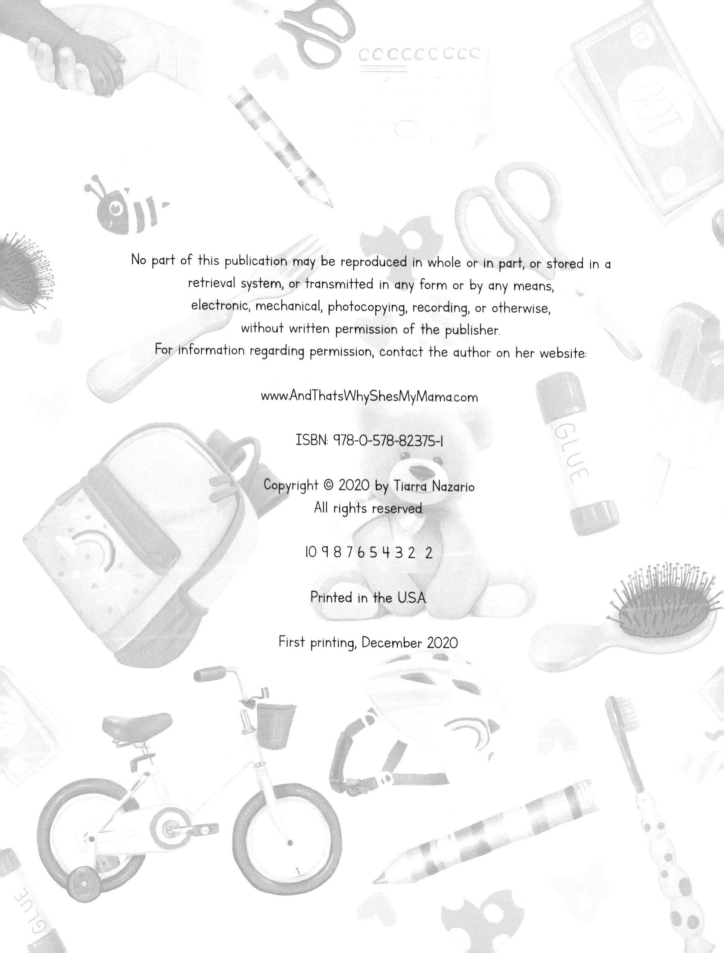

ISBN: 978-0-578-82375-1

10 9 8 7 6 5 4 3 2 2

Printed in the U.S.A.

First printing, December 2020

This book is dedicated with love to all of the Mama's.

I have a special someone who helps me through the day.
She is my mama, which I am happy to say.

In the morning I need help with my teeth and hair.
She makes sure I get all the spots and brush everywhere.

I know I am beautiful inside and out,
from my chin to my feet, my nose and my pout,
my hands, my eyes, my ears and my skin.
But the most beautiful part, is who I am within.

After Mama helps me get ready for the day,
she waves to me and blows a kiss so I can learn and play.

I am **kind** and **respectful** to everyone in school.
I always keep in mind the famous "Golden Rule."

Treating others how I would want them to treat me
makes for the best friend and student I can possibly be.

Sometimes I have homework and even projects to do.
Snip-snip, Mama helps me cut paper, read instructions and squeeze glue.

It doesn't matter if I get an A, B, or C.
As long as I try my best, that's good enough for me.

Everything I do proves I'm **capable** and **smart**.
I'm really **creative** too—I make the most beautiful art.

When the weather is nice, we plan a trip to embark.
It's to one of my favorite places. Can you guess it?
The park!

Back and forth, back and forth. I pump my legs to go high!
I am fun and outstanding as I reach for the sky.

Board games, swings, hide and seek, or tag in the sun,
I love playing with Mama—we laugh and have loads of fun!

As I get older, there is so much to learn.
Mama is there to guide the way as I take each turn.

Sometimes I fall when I try something new,
but getting back up and trying again is the only thing to do.

I am **brave** and **determined** to get it right.
I accomplish my goals, and my future is bright.

Belly aches, a cough, or sniffles—no one likes being sick.
But rest, fluids, and Mama's soup always help do the trick.

She tells me I'll get better soon since I am **powerful** and **strong**.
And guess what she also says? I have been all along.

Mama is never too busy to give an embrace.
She pulls me close and squeezes me right up to her face.

Whether I'm anxious, scared, confused, or mad,
her hugs make me feel safe, special, warm, and glad.

I am **wanted** and **loved** in every single way.
Monday, Tuesday, Wednesday, and each and every day.

She prepares yummy food and puts it in a bowl or plate.

_____ is my favorite. Oh, I cannot wait!
(Insert favorite food here)

Mama puts love and hard work into each and every meal:
season, mix, bake, sauté, measure, pour, and peel.

One bite, two bites, three bites, four!
If I'm still hungry, Mama gives me more.

When I'm finished, I lend a hand and clean up.
I am awesome and helpful. I clear my dish, fork, and cup.

Every once in a while we wish for a treat.
What fun we have when we make cupcakes to eat.

After they cool down, it's time to decorate:
frosting, sprinkles, cherries—oh, I cannot wait!

Just like my cupcake, Mama says I'm **sweet**
I am **nice** and **polite** to everyone I meet.

Most days are great, but some days can be hard.
Mama helps me when I tell her how I feel in the yard.

I am **important** and **wonderful**, I like getting my feelings out.
I can do so and stay calm, there's no need to shout.

I will remember these words for when I feel down,
for I have the ability to turn things around.

Whether I dance, sing, play an instrument, or act,
Mama is there to support me, and that is a fact.

And even when I play sports with my friends outside,
Whether I win or lose—she looks at me with pride.

"Go _____! Go _____!"
(Insert child's name)   (Insert child's name)
I hear her cheering my name.
I'm **happy** to have her by my side
as I have fun playing the game.

Before going to bed, Mama and I sing and read.
She tells me I'm her greatest dream, and I agree.

Then she softly says. . .
"Baby, baby,
I love you.
I'll be here through and through.
Mountains, deserts, rivers blue—
there's no place I wouldn't cross for you!

Your little hands grow bigger every single day.
But even when you're older in my heart you'll stay.
You are unique and incredible, too.
Anything you put your mind to, you can do.

Baby, baby, you fill the world with so much light.
Anytime you need my love I will be here to hold you tight."

All around the world,
there are mamas everywhere.

They take care of their little ones
with tender love and care.

So even though we may look different,
she loves and cherishes me every day.

And that's why she's my mama
in every single way.

Color your beautiful family.